The Vixen

Written by
Stephen Rickard

Illustrated by
Sara Gibbeson

It is a cool night.

Vic and Jeevan can see a fox in the garden.

They can see its tail and its teeth in the moonlight.

Its fur is dark.

Is it a fox or is it a vixen?

Vic tells Jeevan that it is a vixen.

Jeevan gets near the vixen.

The vixen looks up. It can hear Jeevan.

Then the vixen sees Jeevan and Vic.

It runs off down to the river.

The vixen runs near the road.

A van is rushing down the road.

The van is too quick.
The van will hit the vixen.

Vic feels sad.
He sighs and runs into the road.

Jeevan feels sad too.
She is looking for the vixen.

She sees it vanish into the woods.
It is not hurt.

The van did not hit the vixen.

This is good to see.

Will the vixen visit them tonight?